SAVORING LIFE WITH DIABETES

Delicious, Diabetic-Friendly Recipes for Every Meal

RAFFY R. LEOMAH

Copyright © 2024 **RAFFY R. LEOMAH**

All rights reserved. No part of this publication may be reproduced, distributed, or transmitted in any form or by any means, Including photocopying, and recording, or other electronic or mechanical methods, without the prior written permission of the publisher, except in the case of brief quotations embodied in critical reviews and certain other noncommercial uses permitted by copyright law.

TABLE OF CONTENT

Introduction	9
Welcome to Your New Kitchen	9
Chapter 1: Breakfasts to Start Your Day Right	11
Energizing Oatmeal with Berries	11
Ingredients:	11
Instructions:	12
Nutritional Information (Per Serving):	13
Veggie-Packed Scrambled Eggs	13
Ingredients:	14
Instructions:	14
Nutritional Information (Per Serving):	15
Greek Yogurt Parfait with Nuts and Seeds	16
Ingredients:	16
Instructions:	17
Nutritional Information (Per Serving):	18
Whole Grain Pancakes with Fresh Fruit	18
Ingredients:	19
Instructions:	19
Nutritional Information (Per Serving, 3 pancakes):	21
Chapter 2: Satisfying Snacks and Small Bites	22
Crunchy Veggie Sticks with Hummus	22
Ingredients:	22
Instructions:	23
Nutritional Information (Per Serving):	24
Spiced Nuts and Seeds Mix	24

Ingredients:	25
Instructions:	25
Nutritional Information (Per 1/4 Cup Serving):	27
Fresh Fruit Salad with Mint	27
Ingredients:	27
Instructions:	28
Nutritional Information (Per 1 Cup Serving):	29
Low-Carb Smoothies	29
Berry Spinach Smoothie	30
Green Avocado Smoothie	31
Chocolate Peanut Butter Smoothie	32
Chapter 3: Light and Healthy Lunches	**34**
Grilled Chicken and Quinoa Salad	34
Ingredients:	34
Instructions:	35
Nutritional Information (Per Serving, 1 cup salad with 1/2 chicken breast):	36
Mediterranean Chickpea Salad	37
Ingredients:	37
Instructions:	38
Nutritional Information (Per 1 Cup Serving):	39
Zucchini Noodles with Pesto	39
Ingredients:	40
Instructions:	40
Nutritional Information (Per 1 Cup Serving of Zoodles with 2 tablespoons pesto):	41
Turkey and Avocado Wrap	42
Ingredients:	42
Instructions:	43

Nutritional Information (Per Wrap): 43

Chapter 4: Wholesome Dinners for Balanced Blood Sugar 45

Baked Salmon with Asparagus 45
    Ingredients: 45
    Instructions: 45
    Nutritional Information (Per Serving, 1 Salmon Fillet with 1/4 of Asparagus): 47

Stuffed Bell Peppers with Lean Ground Turkey 47
    Ingredients: 48
    Instructions: 48
    Nutritional Information (Per Stuffed Pepper): 50

Cauliflower Rice Stir-Fry with Tofu 50
    Ingredients: 50
    Instructions: 51
    Nutritional Information (Per Serving, 1/4 of the recipe): 52

Herb-Roasted Chicken with Sweet Potatoes 53
    Ingredients: 53
    Instructions: 54
    Nutritional Information (Per Serving, 1 chicken thigh with 1/2 cup sweet potatoes): 55

Chapter 5: Delicious Desserts Without the Guilt 56

Baked Apples with Cinnamon 56
    Ingredients: 56
    Instructions: 56
    Nutritional Information (Per Apple, without additional sweeteners or toppings): 57

Chia Seed Pudding with Fresh Berries 58

Ingredients:	58
Instructions:	59
Nutritional Information (Per Serving, 1/2 cup pudding with berries):	60
Dark Chocolate Almond Bark	60
Ingredients:	60
Instructions:	61
Nutritional Information (Per 1 oz piece):	62
Sugar-Free Lemon Cheesecake	62
Ingredients:	62
Instructions:	63
Nutritional Information (Per Serving, 1/12 of cheesecake):	65

Chapter 6: Beverages to Keep You Hydrated and Healthy — **66**

Herbal Iced Teas	66
Basic Herbal Iced Tea Recipe:	66
Flavor Variations:	67
Nutritional Information (Per 8 oz serving, plain):	68
Freshly Squeezed Lemon Water	68
Ingredients:	69
Instructions:	69
Nutritional Information (Per 8 oz serving):	69
Low-Sugar Smoothies	70
1. Green Berry Smoothie	70
2. Cucumber Melon Smoothie	71
3. Strawberry Basil Smoothie	72
4. Avocado Coconut Smoothie	72

Nutritional Information (Approximate per
   serving, varies by recipe): 73
Spiced Almond Milk 73
   Ingredients: 74
   Instructions: 74
   Nutritional Information (Per 1 cup serving): 75
Conclusion **76**

Introduction

Welcome to Your New Kitchen

Welcome to *"Savoring Life with Diabetes,"* where we believe that managing diabetes doesn't mean sacrificing flavor or enjoyment in your meals. Whether you've been living with diabetes for years or are newly diagnosed, this cookbook is designed to help you create delicious, nutritious meals that support your health and well-being.

The kitchen is the heart of any home, and when you're managing diabetes, it becomes even more important. Here, you'll learn how to transform your kitchen into a space where healthy, diabetic-friendly meals are the norm. We'll guide you through the essentials of stocking your pantry with ingredients that are not only good for your blood sugar but also versatile and full of flavor.

In this introduction, we'll cover the basics of diabetes and nutrition, provide tips on meal planning, and help you understand the key components of a balanced diabetic diet. From learning how to read nutrition labels to discovering new ways to prepare your favorite foods, this section is your gateway to a healthier lifestyle.

Let's embark on this journey together, where every meal is an opportunity to savor life while taking care

of your health. Welcome to your new kitchen—
where delicious, diabetes-friendly meals await!

Chapter 1: Breakfasts to Start Your Day Right

Energizing Oatmeal with Berries

Oatmeal is a fantastic way to start your day, especially when you're managing diabetes. Packed with fiber and slow-digesting carbohydrates, oatmeal helps keep your blood sugar levels stable while providing long-lasting energy. This recipe is enhanced with fresh berries, which add natural sweetness and a boost of antioxidants.

Ingredients:

- 1 cup old-fashioned oats
- 2 cups water or unsweetened almond milk
- 1/2 teaspoon cinnamon
- 1/2 teaspoon vanilla extract (optional)
- 1/2 cup mixed fresh berries (blueberries, strawberries, raspberries)
- 1 tablespoon chia seeds or ground flaxseeds
- 1 tablespoon chopped nuts (almonds, walnuts, or pecans)
- A pinch of salt
- Sweetener of choice (stevia, monk fruit, or a small drizzle of honey, if desired)

Instructions:

1. **Cook the Oats:**
   In a medium saucepan, bring the water or unsweetened almond milk to a boil. Stir in the oats, cinnamon, and a pinch of salt. Reduce heat to low and simmer, stirring occasionally, for about 5-7 minutes or until the oats are tender and have absorbed most of the liquid.
2. **Add Flavorings:**
   Once the oats are cooked, remove the saucepan from the heat. Stir in the vanilla extract, if using, and let the oatmeal sit for a minute to thicken.
3. **Top with Berries and Seeds:**
   Spoon the oatmeal into bowls and top with mixed fresh berries, chia seeds or ground flaxseeds, and chopped nuts. These toppings add a satisfying crunch, healthy fats, and an extra dose of fiber.
4. **Sweeten if Desired:**
   If you prefer a sweeter oatmeal, add a small amount of your preferred sweetener. Remember to use sweeteners sparingly to keep your blood sugar in check.
5. **Serve and Enjoy:**
   Serve the oatmeal warm, and enjoy a nourishing, energizing start to your day.

Nutritional Information (Per Serving):

- **Calories:** ~250
- **Protein:** ~8g
- **Carbohydrates:** ~35g

- **Fiber:** ~8g
- **Sugars:** ~5g (from berries)
- **Fat:** ~10g

This *Energizing Oatmeal with Berries* is not only delicious but also a great way to maintain steady blood sugar levels, providing the energy you need to take on the day. Enjoy it as a wholesome breakfast that supports your health goals while satisfying your taste buds.

Veggie-Packed Scrambled Eggs

Scrambled eggs are a classic breakfast staple, and when loaded with colorful, nutrient-dense vegetables, they become a powerhouse of vitamins, minerals, and protein. This recipe is perfect for those looking to start their day with a low-carb, high-protein meal that keeps blood sugar levels stable and energy levels high.

Ingredients:

- 4 large eggs
- 1/4 cup unsweetened almond milk or water
- 1/2 cup chopped spinach
- 1/4 cup diced bell pepper (any color)
- 1/4 cup diced tomatoes
- 1/4 cup chopped mushrooms
- 2 tablespoons chopped onions

- 1 tablespoon olive oil or cooking spray
- Salt and pepper to taste
- Fresh herbs (optional, such as parsley or chives) for garnish

Instructions:

1. **Prep the Vegetables:**
   Wash and chop the spinach, bell pepper, tomatoes, mushrooms, and onions. Set them aside.
2. **Whisk the Eggs:**
   In a medium bowl, crack the eggs and add the almond milk or water. Whisk until the mixture is well combined and slightly frothy. Season with a pinch of salt and pepper.
3. **Cook the Vegetables:**
   In a large non-stick skillet, heat the olive oil over medium heat. Add the onions and sauté for about 2 minutes, until they begin to soften. Add the bell pepper, mushrooms, and tomatoes, and cook for an additional 3-4 minutes, stirring occasionally, until the vegetables are tender. Finally, add the spinach and cook for another minute, until wilted.
4. **Add the Eggs:**
   Reduce the heat to low and pour the egg mixture over the cooked vegetables. Allow the eggs to cook undisturbed for about 30 seconds, then gently stir the mixture with a spatula, pushing the eggs from the edges toward the center. Continue to cook until the

eggs are set but still slightly creamy, about 2-3 minutes.
5. **Season and Serve:**
Taste and adjust the seasoning with more salt and pepper if needed. Garnish with fresh herbs if desired. Serve immediately and enjoy your veggie-packed scrambled eggs.

Nutritional Information (Per Serving):

- **Calories:** ~200
- **Protein:** ~14g
- **Carbohydrates:** ~5g
- **Fiber:** ~2g
- **Sugars:** ~2g
- **Fat:** ~14g

These *Veggie-Packed Scrambled Eggs* make a satisfying and nutrient-rich breakfast that's quick to prepare. The combination of eggs and vegetables provides a balanced meal full of protein, fiber, and essential vitamins, helping you start your day with a healthy and flavorful dish.

Greek Yogurt Parfait with Nuts and Seeds

A Greek yogurt parfait is a simple yet delightful way to enjoy a nutritious breakfast or snack. By layering creamy Greek yogurt with crunchy nuts, seeds, and a touch of natural sweetness, you create a satisfying dish that's rich in protein, healthy fats, and fiber. This parfait is perfect for those managing diabetes, as it provides a balanced mix of nutrients to help keep blood sugar levels steady.

Ingredients:

- 1 cup plain Greek yogurt (non-fat or low-fat)
- 1/4 cup mixed nuts (almonds, walnuts, pecans), chopped
- 1 tablespoon chia seeds or ground flaxseeds
- 1 tablespoon pumpkin seeds or sunflower seeds
- 1/2 cup fresh berries (such as blueberries, strawberries, or raspberries)
- 1/2 teaspoon vanilla extract (optional)
- Sweetener of choice (stevia, monk fruit, or a small drizzle of honey or maple syrup, if desired)

Instructions:

1. **Prepare the Yogurt:**
   In a small bowl, mix the Greek yogurt with the vanilla extract, if using. This adds a subtle flavor to the yogurt without adding any sugar.
2. **Layer the Parfait:**
   In a glass or bowl, start by spooning half of the Greek yogurt at the bottom. Top with a layer of fresh berries, followed by a sprinkle of chopped nuts, chia seeds, and pumpkin

seeds. Repeat the layers with the remaining yogurt, berries, nuts, and seeds.
3. **Add Sweetener (Optional):**
If you prefer a sweeter parfait, add a small amount of your chosen sweetener. A light drizzle of honey or maple syrup can be used, but it's best to keep this minimal to manage sugar intake.
4. **Serve and Enjoy:**
Serve immediately, or refrigerate for later. The parfait can be made ahead of time for a quick grab-and-go breakfast or snack.

Nutritional Information (Per Serving):

- **Calories:** ~250
- **Protein:** ~18g
- **Carbohydrates:** ~18g
- **Fiber:** ~6g
- **Sugars:** ~8g (from berries)
- **Fat:** ~12g

This *Greek Yogurt Parfait with Nuts and Seeds* is a nutritious option that's quick to assemble and full of flavor. The combination of creamy yogurt, crunchy nuts, and fresh berries makes it a satisfying meal that's both delicious and diabetes-friendly. Enjoy it as a balanced breakfast or a refreshing snack any time of day.

Whole Grain Pancakes with Fresh Fruit

These whole grain pancakes are a delicious way to enjoy a comforting breakfast without spiking your blood sugar. Made with whole grain flour, they are rich in fiber and provide a steady release of energy. Topped with fresh fruit, these pancakes offer natural sweetness and a boost of vitamins, making them a perfect diabetes-friendly option.

Ingredients:

- 1 cup whole wheat flour or oat flour
- 1 tablespoon baking powder
- 1/4 teaspoon salt
- 1 teaspoon cinnamon (optional)
- 1 cup unsweetened almond milk or low-fat milk
- 1 large egg
- 1 tablespoon melted coconut oil or olive oil
- 1 teaspoon vanilla extract
- Cooking spray or a small amount of oil for the pan
- 1 cup fresh fruit (such as blueberries, strawberries, or sliced bananas)

Instructions:

1. **Prepare the Batter:**
   In a large bowl, whisk together the whole wheat flour, baking powder, salt, and

cinnamon. In another bowl, whisk the almond milk, egg, melted coconut oil, and vanilla extract until well combined. Pour the wet ingredients into the dry ingredients and stir until just combined. Be careful not to overmix; the batter should be slightly lumpy.

2. **Cook the Pancakes:**
   Heat a non-stick skillet or griddle over medium heat and lightly grease it with cooking spray or a small amount of oil. Pour 1/4 cup of batter onto the skillet for each pancake. Cook until bubbles form on the surface and the edges look set, about 2-3 minutes. Flip the pancakes and cook for an additional 2-3 minutes, until golden brown and cooked through.
3. **Serve with Fresh Fruit:**
   Stack the pancakes on a plate and top with fresh fruit. The natural sweetness of the fruit complements the hearty flavor of the whole grain pancakes.
4. **Optional Toppings:**
   If desired, add a light drizzle of sugar-free syrup or a sprinkle of chopped nuts for added texture and flavor.
5. **Serve and Enjoy:**
   Serve the pancakes warm and enjoy a satisfying, healthy breakfast.

Nutritional Information (Per Serving, 3 pancakes):

- **Calories:** ~250
- **Protein:** ~8g

- **Carbohydrates:** ~38g
- **Fiber:** ~6g
- **Sugars:** ~8g (from fruit)
- **Fat:** ~8g

These *Whole Grain Pancakes with Fresh Fruit* are a wholesome breakfast choice, providing fiber and nutrients without the sugar spikes that traditional pancakes might cause. Paired with fresh fruit, they are both delicious and supportive of your diabetes management. Enjoy this comforting dish as part of a balanced morning meal!

Chapter 2: Satisfying Snacks and Small Bites

Crunchy Veggie Sticks with Hummus

A perfect snack for any time of day, crunchy veggie sticks paired with creamy hummus offer a satisfying, nutritious option that's low in carbs and high in fiber. This combination not only keeps your blood sugar stable but also provides a variety of vitamins and minerals. Plus, it's a great way to get more vegetables into your diet while enjoying a flavorful dip.

Ingredients:

For the Veggie Sticks:

- 1 large cucumber, cut into sticks
- 2 large carrots, peeled and cut into sticks
- 2 celery stalks, cut into sticks
- 1 red bell pepper, cut into strips
- 1 yellow bell pepper, cut into strips
- 1 handful of cherry tomatoes

For the Hummus:

- 1 can (15 oz) chickpeas, drained and rinsed
- 1/4 cup tahini (sesame seed paste)
- 2 tablespoons olive oil

- 2 tablespoons lemon juice
- 1 garlic clove, minced
- 1/2 teaspoon ground cumin
- 1/4 teaspoon salt (or to taste)
- 2-3 tablespoons water (to reach desired consistency)
- Paprika and olive oil for garnish (optional)

Instructions:

1. **Prepare the Veggie Sticks:**
   Wash and cut the cucumber, carrots, celery, and bell peppers into sticks. Arrange the veggie sticks and cherry tomatoes on a large platter or in individual serving cups.
2. **Make the Hummus:**
   In a food processor, combine the chickpeas, tahini, olive oil, lemon juice, garlic, cumin, and salt. Blend until smooth, adding water a tablespoon at a time until the hummus reaches your desired consistency. Taste and adjust the seasoning if needed.
3. **Serve the Hummus:**
   Spoon the hummus into a serving bowl and drizzle with a little olive oil and a sprinkle of paprika, if desired.
4. **Dip and Enjoy:**
   Serve the veggie sticks alongside the hummus. Dip the crunchy vegetables into the creamy hummus for a satisfying, nutrient-rich snack.

Nutritional Information (Per Serving):

- **Calories:** ~150
- **Protein:** ~5g
- **Carbohydrates:** ~15g
- **Fiber:** ~5g
- **Sugars:** ~5g (from vegetables)
- **Fat:** ~8g

This *Crunchy Veggie Sticks with Hummus* snack is a delicious and healthy way to enjoy a variety of fresh vegetables with a protein-packed dip. The fiber from the veggies and the protein from the hummus make this snack filling and perfect for keeping your energy levels stable throughout the day.

Spiced Nuts and Seeds Mix

This spiced nuts and seeds mix is a perfect snack for those moments when you need something crunchy and savory. Packed with healthy fats, protein, and fiber, this mix will keep you satisfied and energized while helping to manage your blood sugar levels. It's easy to make and perfect for on-the-go snacking or as a topping for salads and yogurt.

Ingredients:

- 1/2 cup raw almonds
- 1/2 cup raw walnuts

- 1/4 cup raw pumpkin seeds
- 1/4 cup raw sunflower seeds
- 2 tablespoons chia seeds or flaxseeds
- 1 tablespoon olive oil or coconut oil
- 1 teaspoon ground cinnamon
- 1/2 teaspoon ground cumin
- 1/2 teaspoon smoked paprika (or regular paprika)
- 1/4 teaspoon ground cayenne pepper (optional, for a bit of heat)
- 1/2 teaspoon sea salt
- 1/4 teaspoon black pepper

Instructions:

1. **Preheat the Oven:**
   Preheat your oven to 325°F (160°C) and line a baking sheet with parchment paper.
2. **Mix the Nuts and Seeds:**
   In a large bowl, combine the almonds, walnuts, pumpkin seeds, sunflower seeds, and chia seeds (or flaxseeds).
3. **Add the Spices:**
   Drizzle the olive oil or coconut oil over the nuts and seeds. Sprinkle in the cinnamon, cumin, paprika, cayenne pepper (if using), sea salt, and black pepper. Toss everything together until the nuts and seeds are evenly coated with the oil and spices.
4. **Bake the Mix:**
   Spread the nut and seed mixture in an even layer on the prepared baking sheet. Bake in the preheated oven for 15-20 minutes,

stirring once halfway through, until the nuts are golden and fragrant. Be careful not to overcook, as nuts can burn quickly.
5. **Cool and Store:**
Remove the baking sheet from the oven and let the mix cool completely. Once cooled, transfer the spiced nuts and seeds to an airtight container. Store at room temperature for up to two weeks.
6. **Serve and Enjoy:**
Enjoy this spiced nuts and seeds mix as a snack, or sprinkle it over salads, yogurt, or oatmeal for added crunch and flavor.

Nutritional Information (Per 1/4 Cup Serving):

- **Calories:** ~200
- **Protein:** ~5g
- **Carbohydrates:** ~5g
- **Fiber:** ~3g
- **Sugars:** ~1g
- **Fat:** ~18g

This *Spiced Nuts and Seeds Mix* is a satisfying and nutritious snack that's rich in healthy fats and packed with flavor. It's a great way to curb hunger while managing blood sugar, making it an ideal choice for anyone looking to maintain a healthy, balanced diet.

Fresh Fruit Salad with Mint

This fresh fruit salad is a refreshing and vibrant way to enjoy a variety of fruits. The addition of mint adds a burst of flavor that complements the natural sweetness of the fruit, making it a perfect side dish or light dessert. It's low in calories and high in vitamins, fiber, and antioxidants, ideal for managing blood sugar levels while satisfying your sweet tooth.

Ingredients:

- 1 cup fresh strawberries, hulled and sliced
- 1 cup blueberries
- 1 cup cubed cantaloupe or honeydew melon
- 1 cup diced pineapple
- 1 apple, cored and diced
- 1 kiwi, peeled and sliced
- 1 tablespoon fresh mint leaves, finely chopped
- 1 tablespoon lemon juice
- 1 teaspoon honey or a pinch of stevia (optional, for added sweetness)

Instructions:

1. **Prepare the Fruit:**
   Wash and prepare all the fruit. Slice the strawberries, cube the melon, dice the pineapple and apple, and slice the kiwi.
2. **Combine the Fruit:**
   In a large bowl, gently combine all the prepared fruit.

3. **Add Mint and Lemon Juice:**
   Sprinkle the chopped mint over the fruit. Drizzle with lemon juice and, if desired, add a teaspoon of honey or a pinch of stevia for extra sweetness. Gently toss everything together to coat the fruit evenly with the mint and lemon juice.
4. **Chill and Serve:**
   Refrigerate the fruit salad for about 30 minutes to allow the flavors to meld. Serve chilled as a refreshing snack, side dish, or light dessert.

Nutritional Information (Per 1 Cup Serving):

- **Calories:** ~80
- **Protein:** ~1g
- **Carbohydrates:** ~20g
- **Fiber:** ~3g
- **Sugars:** ~15g (from fruit)
- **Fat:** ~0.5g

This *Fresh Fruit Salad with Mint* is a delightful way to enjoy a variety of fresh, seasonal fruits while keeping your snack or meal both healthy and satisfying. The mint adds a refreshing twist that makes this salad even more enjoyable.

Low-Carb Smoothies

Low-carb smoothies are a fantastic way to enjoy a nutritious and filling beverage without spiking your blood sugar. These smoothies use low-carb ingredients while still providing plenty of flavor and essential nutrients. They're perfect for breakfast, a snack, or even a light meal.

Berry Spinach Smoothie

Ingredients:

- 1 cup unsweetened almond milk or low-fat milk
- 1 cup fresh spinach leaves
- 1/2 cup mixed berries (strawberries, raspberries, blueberries)
- 1 tablespoon chia seeds or flaxseeds
- 1/2 avocado
- 1/2 teaspoon vanilla extract (optional)
- Ice cubes (optional)

Instructions:

1. **Blend Ingredients:**
   Combine all ingredients in a blender. Blend until smooth, adding ice cubes if desired for a thicker consistency.
2. **Serve:**
   Pour into a glass and enjoy immediately.

Nutritional Information (Per Serving):

- **Calories:** ~180

- **Protein:** ~4g
- **Carbohydrates:** ~15g
- **Fiber:** ~7g
- **Sugars:** ~6g
- **Fat:** ~12g

Green Avocado Smoothie

Ingredients:

- 1 cup unsweetened almond milk or low-fat milk
- 1/2 avocado
- 1/2 cucumber, peeled and chopped
- 1 cup kale or spinach leaves
- 1 tablespoon chia seeds or hemp seeds
- Juice of 1/2 lemon
- Ice cubes (optional)

Instructions:

1. **Blend Ingredients:**
   Add all ingredients to a blender and blend until smooth. Add ice cubes for a thicker texture if desired.
2. **Serve:**
   Pour into a glass and enjoy right away.

Nutritional Information (Per Serving):

- **Calories:** ~190
- **Protein:** ~5g
- **Carbohydrates:** ~12g

- **Fiber:** ~8g
- **Sugars:** ~4g
- **Fat:** ~14g

Chocolate Peanut Butter Smoothie

Ingredients:

- 1 cup unsweetened almond milk or low-fat milk
- 1 tablespoon unsweetened cocoa powder
- 1 tablespoon natural peanut butter (or almond butter)
- 1/2 avocado
- 1 tablespoon chia seeds or flaxseeds
- A few ice cubes

Instructions:

1. **Blend Ingredients:**
   Combine all ingredients in a blender and blend until smooth, adding ice cubes for a thicker texture if desired.
2. **Serve:**
   Pour into a glass and enjoy.

Nutritional Information (Per Serving):

- **Calories:** ~220
- **Protein:** ~7g
- **Carbohydrates:** ~12g
- **Fiber:** ~7g
- **Sugars:** ~3g

- **Fat:** ~16g

These *Low-Carb Smoothies* are not only delicious but also tailored to support stable blood sugar levels while delivering essential nutrients. Enjoy these smoothies as part of a balanced diet to keep your energy levels steady and your cravings in check.

Chapter 3: Light and Healthy Lunches

Grilled Chicken and Quinoa Salad

This Grilled Chicken and Quinoa Salad is a nutritious and satisfying meal that's perfect for lunch or dinner. The combination of lean chicken, protein-packed quinoa, and fresh vegetables provides a balanced mix of protein, fiber, and vitamins, making it ideal for managing blood sugar levels.

Ingredients:

For the Salad:

- 1 cup quinoa, rinsed
- 2 cups water or low-sodium chicken broth
- 2 boneless, skinless chicken breasts
- 1 tablespoon olive oil
- 1 teaspoon paprika
- 1/2 teaspoon garlic powder
- 1/2 teaspoon dried oregano
- Salt and pepper to taste
- 1 cup cherry tomatoes, halved
- 1/2 cucumber, diced
- 1/4 red onion, finely chopped
- 1/2 cup diced bell pepper (any color)
- 1/4 cup fresh parsley, chopped

For the Dressing:

- 2 tablespoons olive oil
- 1 tablespoon lemon juice
- 1 teaspoon Dijon mustard
- 1 garlic clove, minced
- Salt and pepper to taste

Instructions:

1. **Cook the Quinoa:**
   In a medium saucepan, bring the water or chicken broth to a boil. Add the quinoa, reduce heat to low, cover, and simmer for 15 minutes, or until the quinoa is tender and the liquid is absorbed. Fluff with a fork and let it cool.
2. **Prepare the Chicken:**
   Preheat your grill or a grill pan over medium-high heat. Rub the chicken breasts with olive oil, paprika, garlic powder, oregano, salt, and pepper. Grill the chicken for about 6-7 minutes per side, or until fully cooked and the internal temperature reaches 165°F (74°C). Remove from the grill and let the chicken rest for 5 minutes before slicing.
3. **Assemble the Salad:**
   In a large bowl, combine the cooked quinoa, cherry tomatoes, cucumber, red onion, bell pepper, and parsley. Toss to mix.
4. **Make the Dressing:**
   In a small bowl, whisk together the olive oil,

lemon juice, Dijon mustard, minced garlic, salt, and pepper.
5. **Combine and Serve:**
Pour the dressing over the salad and toss to coat evenly. Slice the grilled chicken and place it on top of the salad. Serve immediately, or chill in the refrigerator for up to 2 hours before serving.

Nutritional Information (Per Serving, 1 cup salad with 1/2 chicken breast):

- **Calories:** ~300
- **Protein:** ~25g
- **Carbohydrates:** ~25g
- **Fiber:** ~5g
- **Sugars:** ~4g
- **Fat:** ~12g

This *Grilled Chicken and Quinoa Salad* is a well-rounded meal that's both filling and healthy. The lean protein from the chicken and the fiber from the quinoa and vegetables make it a great choice for maintaining stable blood sugar levels and promoting overall health.

Mediterranean Chickpea Salad

This Mediterranean Chickpea Salad is a flavorful and nutritious dish that combines the wholesome goodness of chickpeas with fresh vegetables and a zesty dressing. It's perfect for a quick lunch, a light dinner, or as a side dish. Rich in protein and fiber, this salad is also great for managing blood sugar levels.

Ingredients:

For the Salad:

- 1 can (15 oz) chickpeas, drained and rinsed
- 1 cup cherry tomatoes, halved
- 1/2 cucumber, diced
- 1/4 red onion, finely chopped
- 1/4 cup kalamata olives, pitted and sliced
- 1/4 cup crumbled feta cheese (optional)
- 1/4 cup fresh parsley, chopped
- 2 tablespoons fresh basil or mint, chopped (optional)

For the Dressing:

- 3 tablespoons olive oil
- 2 tablespoons lemon juice
- 1 tablespoon red wine vinegar
- 1 teaspoon Dijon mustard
- 1 garlic clove, minced
- 1/2 teaspoon dried oregano
- Salt and pepper to taste

Instructions:

1. **Prepare the Salad Ingredients:**
   In a large bowl, combine the chickpeas,

cherry tomatoes, cucumber, red onion, olives, feta cheese (if using), and parsley. Add the basil or mint if desired.
2. **Make the Dressing:**
In a small bowl, whisk together the olive oil, lemon juice, red wine vinegar, Dijon mustard, minced garlic, dried oregano, salt, and pepper.
3. **Combine and Toss:**
Pour the dressing over the salad and toss to coat all the ingredients evenly.
4. **Serve:**
Serve the salad immediately, or refrigerate for 30 minutes to allow the flavors to meld. This salad can be enjoyed chilled or at room temperature.

Nutritional Information (Per 1 Cup Serving):

- **Calories:** ~180
- **Protein:** ~6g
- **Carbohydrates:** ~20g
- **Fiber:** ~6g
- **Sugars:** ~5g
- **Fat:** ~9g

This *Mediterranean Chickpea Salad* is a vibrant and satisfying dish that's rich in nutrients and flavor. The combination of chickpeas, fresh vegetables, and a tangy dressing makes it a delicious and healthy option for anyone looking to enjoy a balanced, diabetes-friendly meal.

Zucchini Noodles with Pesto

Zucchini noodles, or "zoodles," are a fantastic low-carb alternative to traditional pasta. When paired with a flavorful homemade pesto, this dish becomes a light yet satisfying meal that's perfect for anyone managing their blood sugar levels. The fresh basil and nuts in the pesto add a rich taste without the extra carbs.

Ingredients:

For the Zucchini Noodles:

- 3 medium zucchinis
- 1 tablespoon olive oil
- Salt and pepper to taste

For the Pesto:

- 2 cups fresh basil leaves
- 1/4 cup pine nuts or walnuts
- 1/4 cup grated Parmesan cheese (optional)
- 2 garlic cloves
- 1/4 cup olive oil
- Juice of 1/2 lemon
- Salt and pepper to taste

Instructions:

1. **Prepare the Zucchini Noodles:**
   Use a spiralizer or julienne peeler to create noodles from the zucchinis. If using a spiralizer, follow the manufacturer's instructions. If using a julienne peeler, peel the zucchini into thin strips.
2. **Cook the Zoodles:**
   Heat olive oil in a large skillet over medium heat. Add the zucchini noodles and sauté for 3-4 minutes, until they are tender but still have a bit of crunch. Season with salt and pepper. Remove from heat.
3. **Make the Pesto:**
   In a food processor, combine the basil, pine nuts or walnuts, Parmesan cheese (if using), and garlic. Pulse until the mixture is finely chopped. With the processor running, slowly add the olive oil until the pesto is smooth and creamy. Add lemon juice, salt, and pepper to taste.
4. **Combine and Serve:**
   Toss the cooked zucchini noodles with the pesto until they are well coated. Serve immediately, or chill for later use.

Nutritional Information (Per 1 Cup Serving of Zoodles with 2 tablespoons pesto):

- **Calories:** ~150
- **Protein:** ~4g
- **Carbohydrates:** ~7g
- **Fiber:** ~2g
- **Sugars:** ~4g

- **Fat:** ~13g

This *Zucchini Noodles with Pesto* dish is a delicious, low-carb alternative to traditional pasta dishes. The zucchini provides a satisfying texture, while the pesto adds a burst of fresh, herbaceous flavor, making it a great option for a healthy, diabetes-friendly meal.

Turkey and Avocado Wrap

This Turkey and Avocado Wrap is a quick, nutritious meal that's easy to prepare and packed with flavor. It combines lean turkey with creamy avocado and fresh vegetables, all wrapped up in a low-carb tortilla. This wrap is perfect for a satisfying lunch or a light dinner, providing a balanced mix of protein, healthy fats, and fiber.

Ingredients:

- 1 large low-carb tortilla or whole grain wrap
- 4 slices of lean turkey breast (or 4 oz shredded turkey)
- 1/2 ripe avocado, sliced
- 1/2 cup fresh spinach or mixed greens
- 1/4 cup sliced cherry tomatoes
- 1/4 cucumber, sliced
- 1 tablespoon hummus or Greek yogurt (optional, for spreading)

- 1 tablespoon Dijon mustard or your preferred low-carb dressing (optional)
- Salt and pepper to taste

Instructions:

1. **Prepare the Wrap:**
   Lay the tortilla flat on a clean surface. If using, spread a thin layer of hummus or Greek yogurt on the tortilla, and/or a layer of Dijon mustard or your preferred dressing.
2. **Layer Ingredients:**
   Arrange the spinach or mixed greens in the center of the tortilla. Place the turkey slices on top of the greens. Add the avocado slices, cherry tomatoes, and cucumber.
3. **Season and Roll:**
   Season with salt and pepper to taste. Carefully roll up the tortilla tightly, folding in the sides as you go to secure the filling.
4. **Serve:**
   Slice the wrap in half if desired, and serve immediately.

Nutritional Information (Per Wrap):

- **Calories:** ~350
- **Protein:** ~25g
- **Carbohydrates:** ~20g
- **Fiber:** ~8g
- **Sugars:** ~4g
- **Fat:** ~20g

This *Turkey and Avocado Wrap* is a balanced meal that combines lean protein with healthy fats and plenty of vegetables. It's easy to make and perfect for a quick, nutritious lunch or dinner.

Chapter 4: Wholesome Dinners for Balanced Blood Sugar

Baked Salmon with Asparagus

This Baked Salmon with Asparagus is a simple and elegant meal that's both healthy and delicious. Salmon is rich in omega-3 fatty acids and paired with asparagus, it makes for a nutrient-dense dinner that's easy to prepare and perfect for managing blood sugar levels.

Ingredients:

- 4 salmon fillets (6 oz each), skin-on or skinless
- 1 bunch fresh asparagus, trimmed
- 2 tablespoons olive oil
- 1 lemon, sliced
- 3 cloves garlic, minced
- 1 teaspoon dried thyme or rosemary
- Salt and pepper to taste
- Lemon wedges for serving (optional)

Instructions:

1. **Preheat the Oven:**
   Preheat your oven to 400°F (200°C). Line a baking sheet with parchment paper or lightly grease it with cooking spray.

2. **Prepare the Salmon and Asparagus:**
Place the salmon fillets on one side of the prepared baking sheet. Arrange the asparagus on the other side of the baking sheet.
3. **Season and Drizzle:**
Drizzle the olive oil over both the salmon and asparagus. Season the salmon with minced garlic, dried thyme or rosemary, salt, and pepper. Toss the asparagus with a bit of salt and pepper.
4. **Add Lemon:**
Place lemon slices on top of the salmon fillets. You can also squeeze a bit of lemon juice over the asparagus if you like.
5. **Bake:**
Bake in the preheated oven for 12-15 minutes, or until the salmon is cooked through and flakes easily with a fork and the asparagus is tender and slightly crisp.
6. **Serve:**
Remove from the oven and let rest for a few minutes. Serve the salmon fillets with the roasted asparagus and extra lemon wedges if desired.

Nutritional Information (Per Serving, 1 Salmon Fillet with 1/4 of Asparagus):

- **Calories:** ~300
- **Protein:** ~30g
- **Carbohydrates:** ~8g
- **Fiber:** ~4g

- **Sugars:** ~3g
- **Fat:** ~15g

This *Baked Salmon with Asparagus* is a delicious, low-carb meal that's easy to make and packed with nutrients. The combination of flavorful salmon and tender asparagus makes for a satisfying dish that's great for maintaining stable blood sugar levels and supporting overall health.

Stuffed Bell Peppers with Lean Ground Turkey

These Stuffed Bell Peppers with Lean Ground Turkey are a nutritious and satisfying meal. Packed with lean protein, vegetables, and spices, they offer a balanced and delicious way to enjoy a low-carb and high-fiber dish.

Ingredients:

- 4 large bell peppers (any color)
- 1 lb (450g) lean ground turkey
- 1 small onion, finely chopped
- 2 cloves garlic, minced
- 1 cup diced tomatoes (canned or fresh)
- 1/2 cup cooked quinoa or brown rice (optional for added texture)
- 1 cup spinach or kale, chopped
- 1 teaspoon dried oregano

- 1/2 teaspoon ground cumin
- 1/2 teaspoon smoked paprika
- Salt and pepper to taste
- 1/2 cup shredded mozzarella cheese or cheddar cheese (optional)
- 1 tablespoon olive oil

Instructions:

1. **Preheat the Oven:**
   Preheat your oven to 375°F (190°C).
2. **Prepare the Bell Peppers:**
   Cut the tops off the bell peppers and remove the seeds and membranes. Set aside.
3. **Cook the Filling:**
   Heat olive oil in a large skillet over medium heat. Add the chopped onion and garlic and cook until softened, about 3-4 minutes. Add the ground turkey and cook until browned and cooked through, breaking it up with a spoon. Stir in the diced tomatoes, cooked quinoa or brown rice (if using), chopped spinach or kale, oregano, cumin, paprika, salt, and pepper. Cook for an additional 5 minutes until everything is well combined and heated through.
4. **Stuff the Peppers:**
   Spoon the turkey mixture into the prepared bell peppers, packing it in tightly. Place the stuffed peppers upright in a baking dish.
5. **Bake:**
   If using cheese, sprinkle the shredded cheese on top of each stuffed pepper. Cover

the baking dish with foil and bake in the preheated oven for 30 minutes. Remove the foil and bake for an additional 10 minutes, or until the peppers are tender and the cheese is melted and bubbly.
6. **Serve:**
Remove from the oven and let the peppers cool slightly before serving.

Nutritional Information (Per Stuffed Pepper):

- **Calories:** ~300
- **Protein:** ~25g
- **Carbohydrates:** ~20g (including optional quinoa or rice)
- **Fiber:** ~6g
- **Sugars:** ~8g
- **Fat:** ~12g

These *Stuffed Bell Peppers with Lean Ground Turkey* are a great option for a healthy, balanced meal. They provide a good mix of protein and vegetables, making them a delicious choice for anyone looking to maintain stable blood sugar levels.

Cauliflower Rice Stir-Fry with Tofu

This Cauliflower Rice Stir-Fry with Tofu is a low-carb, vegetarian meal that's full of flavor and texture. It uses cauliflower rice as a low-carb alternative to traditional rice and includes tofu for a protein boost, making it a healthy and satisfying option.

Ingredients:

- 1 large head of cauliflower, riced (about 4 cups)
- 1 block (14 oz) firm tofu, drained and cubed
- 2 tablespoons sesame oil or olive oil
- 1 cup bell peppers, diced (any color)
- 1 cup broccoli florets
- 1/2 cup carrots, sliced
- 1/2 cup snap peas or green beans
- 2 cloves garlic, minced
- 1 tablespoon fresh ginger, minced
- 3 tablespoons low-sodium soy sauce or tamari
- 1 tablespoon rice vinegar
- 1 tablespoon hoisin sauce (optional, for added sweetness)
- 2 green onions, chopped (for garnish)
- 1 tablespoon sesame seeds (for garnish)

Instructions:

1. **Prepare the Tofu:**
   Heat 1 tablespoon of sesame oil in a large skillet or wok over medium-high heat. Add the cubed tofu and cook until golden brown and crispy on all sides, about 8-10 minutes. Remove tofu from the skillet and set aside.

2. **Cook the Vegetables:**
   In the same skillet, add the remaining 1 tablespoon of sesame oil. Add the garlic and ginger and cook for 30 seconds until fragrant. Add the bell peppers, broccoli, carrots, and snap peas. Stir-fry for 5-7 minutes until the vegetables are tender but still crisp.
3. **Add the Cauliflower Rice:**
   Add the riced cauliflower to the skillet with the vegetables. Stir to combine and cook for another 5 minutes, allowing the cauliflower to become tender.
4. **Season the Stir-Fry:**
   Return the tofu to the skillet. Add the soy sauce, rice vinegar, and hoisin sauce (if using). Stir everything together and cook for another 2-3 minutes until heated through and well combined.
5. **Garnish and Serve:**
   Remove from heat and garnish with chopped green onions and sesame seeds. Serve hot.

Nutritional Information (Per Serving, 1/4 of the recipe):

- **Calories:** ~250
- **Protein:** ~15g
- **Carbohydrates:** ~20g
- **Fiber:** ~6g
- **Sugars:** ~6g
- **Fat:** ~15g

This *Cauliflower Rice Stir-Fry with Tofu* is a flavorful and filling dish that's low in carbs and rich in nutrients. The combination of tofu and a variety of vegetables makes it a well-rounded meal that's perfect for managing blood sugar and maintaining a healthy diet.

Herb-Roasted Chicken with Sweet Potatoes

This Herb-Roasted Chicken with Sweet Potatoes is a hearty and flavorful meal that's easy to prepare. The roasted chicken is seasoned with a blend of herbs, and the sweet potatoes add a touch of natural sweetness and additional nutrients. It's a balanced and satisfying dish perfect for any meal.

Ingredients:

- 4 bone-in, skin-on chicken thighs or breasts
- 2 large sweet potatoes, peeled and cut into chunks
- 2 tablespoons olive oil
- 1 tablespoon fresh rosemary, chopped (or 1 teaspoon dried)
- 1 tablespoon fresh thyme, chopped (or 1 teaspoon dried)
- 4 cloves garlic, minced
- 1 lemon, sliced
- Salt and pepper to taste

- 1/2 teaspoon paprika (optional, for extra flavor)
- Fresh parsley for garnish (optional)

Instructions:

1. **Preheat the Oven:**
   Preheat your oven to 400°F (200°C). Line a baking sheet with parchment paper or lightly grease it.
2. **Prepare the Chicken and Sweet Potatoes:**
   Place the chicken thighs or breasts and sweet potato chunks on the baking sheet. Drizzle with olive oil. Season the chicken and sweet potatoes with rosemary, thyme, minced garlic, salt, pepper, and paprika (if using). Toss the sweet potatoes to coat them evenly.
3. **Add Lemon:**
   Place lemon slices on top of the chicken and scatter a few around the sweet potatoes.
4. **Roast:**
   Roast in the preheated oven for 35-40 minutes, or until the chicken is cooked through and reaches an internal temperature of 165°F (74°C), and the sweet potatoes are tender. If you want the chicken skin extra crispy, you can broil for an additional 2-3 minutes at the end.
5. **Serve:**
   Remove from the oven and let rest for a few minutes. Garnish with fresh parsley if

desired. Serve the chicken with the roasted sweet potatoes.

Nutritional Information (Per Serving, 1 chicken thigh with 1/2 cup sweet potatoes):

- **Calories:** ~350
- **Protein:** ~25g
- **Carbohydrates:** ~30g
- **Fiber:** ~4g
- **Sugars:** ~8g
- **Fat:** ~15g

This *Herb-Roasted Chicken with Sweet Potatoes* is a wholesome, balanced meal that's rich in flavor and nutrients. The combination of lean chicken and sweet potatoes makes it a satisfying and healthy option for maintaining stable blood sugar levels.

Chapter 5: Delicious Desserts Without the Guilt

Baked Apples with Cinnamon

Baked Apples with Cinnamon are a simple and comforting dessert that's both nutritious and low in added sugars. This recipe brings out the natural sweetness of the apples and pairs it with aromatic cinnamon for a warm and satisfying treat.

Ingredients:

- 4 medium apples (such as Honeycrisp, Gala, or Fuji)
- 1/4 cup chopped nuts (such as walnuts or pecans, optional)
- 1/4 cup raisins or dried cranberries (optional)
- 1 tablespoon honey or maple syrup (optional, for extra sweetness)
- 1 teaspoon ground cinnamon
- 1/4 teaspoon ground nutmeg (optional)
- 1/4 cup water

Instructions:

1. **Preheat the Oven:**
   Preheat your oven to 350°F (175°C).
2. **Prepare the Apples:**
   Core the apples, creating a cavity in the

center. You can use an apple corer or a paring knife.
3. **Stuff the Apples:**
In a small bowl, mix the chopped nuts, raisins or dried cranberries (if using), and half of the ground cinnamon. If desired, stir in the honey or maple syrup. Stuff this mixture into the cavity of each apple.
4. **Season and Bake:**
Place the stuffed apples in a baking dish. Sprinkle the remaining cinnamon and nutmeg (if using) over the apples. Pour the water into the bottom of the baking dish to help keep the apples moist while baking.
5. **Bake:**
Bake in the preheated oven for 30-35 minutes, or until the apples are tender and slightly caramelized.
6. **Serve:**
Allow the apples to cool slightly before serving. They can be enjoyed warm as is or with a dollop of Greek yogurt or a sprinkle of granola for added texture.

Nutritional Information (Per Apple, without additional sweeteners or toppings):

- **Calories:** ~90
- **Protein:** ~0.5g
- **Carbohydrates:** ~24g
- **Fiber:** ~4g
- **Sugars:** ~18g (naturally occurring from apples)

- **Fat:** ~0.5g

These *Baked Apples with Cinnamon* offer a naturally sweet and comforting dessert that's easy to prepare. The apples become tender and flavorful while retaining their natural nutrients, making this a healthy choice for a light treat.

Chia Seed Pudding with Fresh Berries

Chia Seed Pudding with Fresh Berries is a nutritious and versatile dessert or breakfast option. It's packed with fiber, protein, and healthy fats, and topped with fresh berries for added flavor and nutrients.

Ingredients:

- 1/4 cup chia seeds
- 1 cup unsweetened almond milk (or any preferred milk)
- 1 tablespoon honey or maple syrup (optional, for added sweetness)
- 1/2 teaspoon vanilla extract
- Fresh berries (such as strawberries, blueberries, or raspberries) for topping

Instructions:

1. **Combine Ingredients:**
   In a medium bowl, whisk together the chia seeds, almond milk, honey or maple syrup (if using), and vanilla extract.
2. **Chill and Set:**
   Cover the bowl and refrigerate for at least 4 hours, or overnight. The chia seeds will absorb the liquid and form a thick, pudding-like consistency.
3. **Stir and Serve:**
   Before serving, stir the pudding well to ensure an even texture. Spoon the pudding into serving dishes or bowls.
4. **Top with Berries:**
   Top each serving with fresh berries. You can also add a sprinkle of nuts, seeds, or a dollop of Greek yogurt if desired.

Nutritional Information (Per Serving, 1/2 cup pudding with berries):

- **Calories:** ~150
- **Protein:** ~5g
- **Carbohydrates:** ~20g
- **Fiber:** ~10g
- **Sugars:** ~7g (varies depending on berries and sweetener)
- **Fat:** ~7g

This *Chia Seed Pudding with Fresh Berries* is a delicious and healthy option that provides a good balance of protein, fiber, and healthy fats. It's perfect for a quick breakfast or a satisfying dessert.

Dark Chocolate Almond Bark

Dark Chocolate Almond Bark is a simple and elegant treat that's perfect for satisfying your sweet tooth while keeping things relatively healthy. Made with high-quality dark chocolate and almonds, it's a delicious way to enjoy a low-sugar snack or dessert.

Ingredients:

- 8 oz (225g) dark chocolate (70% cocoa or higher), chopped
- 1 cup whole almonds, toasted
- Sea salt (optional, for sprinkling)

Instructions:

1. **Melt the Chocolate:**
   In a heatproof bowl, melt the dark chocolate over a pot of simmering water (double boiler method) or in the microwave in 20-30 second intervals, stirring in between until smooth.
2. **Prepare the Bark:**
   Line a baking sheet with parchment paper. Once the chocolate is melted, stir in the toasted almonds.
3. **Spread and Set:**
   Pour the chocolate and almond mixture onto the prepared baking sheet. Spread it out into

an even layer using a spatula. If desired, sprinkle a pinch of sea salt over the top for extra flavor.
4. **Chill:**
Refrigerate the bark for about 30 minutes, or until it is completely set and hardened.
5. **Break and Serve:**
Once set, break the bark into pieces and store in an airtight container in the refrigerator.

Nutritional Information (Per 1 oz piece):

- **Calories:** ~150
- **Protein:** ~3g
- **Carbohydrates:** ~10g
- **Fiber:** ~3g
- **Sugars:** ~6g
- **Fat:** ~12g

This *Dark Chocolate Almond Bark* is a rich and satisfying treat that combines the antioxidants of dark chocolate with the crunch of almonds. It's a great way to enjoy a sweet snack while still making a healthier choice.

Sugar-Free Lemon Cheesecake

This Sugar-Free Lemon Cheesecake is a creamy and refreshing dessert that's perfect for those who are watching their sugar intake. With a tangy lemon flavor and a smooth texture, it's a satisfying treat that fits into a healthy lifestyle.

Ingredients:

For the Crust:

- 1 1/2 cups almond flour
- 1/4 cup melted butter or coconut oil
- 2 tablespoons erythritol or another sugar substitute
- 1/4 teaspoon vanilla extract

For the Filling:

- 16 oz (450g) cream cheese, softened
- 1 cup Greek yogurt or sour cream
- 1/2 cup erythritol or another sugar substitute
- 1/4 cup lemon juice (freshly squeezed)
- 2 teaspoons lemon zest
- 3 large eggs
- 1 teaspoon vanilla extract

Instructions:

1. **Preheat the Oven:**
   Preheat your oven to 325°F (163°C). Grease a 9-inch springform pan.
2. **Prepare the Crust:**
   In a medium bowl, mix together the almond flour, melted butter or coconut oil, erythritol, and vanilla extract until well combined. Press

the mixture evenly into the bottom of the prepared springform pan. Bake for 10 minutes, then remove from the oven and let cool slightly.
3. **Prepare the Filling:**
In a large mixing bowl, beat the cream cheese until smooth and creamy. Add the Greek yogurt, erythritol, lemon juice, lemon zest, and vanilla extract. Mix until well combined. Add the eggs one at a time, mixing on low speed after each addition until just combined.
4. **Bake the Cheesecake:**
Pour the cream cheese mixture over the cooled crust in the springform pan. Smooth the top with a spatula. Bake in the preheated oven for 50-60 minutes, or until the center is set and the edges are lightly golden. The center should still have a slight jiggle.
5. **Cool and Chill:**
Turn off the oven and crack the oven door slightly. Let the cheesecake cool in the oven for 1 hour. Remove from the oven and refrigerate for at least 4 hours, or overnight, to fully set.
6. **Serve:**
Before serving, you can garnish with extra lemon zest or a few fresh berries if desired.

Nutritional Information (Per Serving, 1/12 of cheesecake):

- **Calories:** ~230

- **Protein:** ~7g
- **Carbohydrates:** ~8g
- **Fiber:** ~2g
- **Sugars:** ~1g (naturally occurring)
- **Fat:** ~19g

This *Sugar-Free Lemon Cheesecake* provides a creamy, lemony flavor without the added sugars, making it a delicious and satisfying option for a low-carb or sugar-free diet.

Chapter 6: Beverages to Keep You Hydrated and Healthy

Herbal Iced Teas

Herbal iced teas are refreshing and versatile, making them perfect for a cool drink any time of the year. They're naturally caffeine-free and can be enjoyed plain or sweetened with your preferred sugar substitute. Here are a few variations to try:

Basic Herbal Iced Tea Recipe:

Ingredients:

- 4-6 herbal tea bags (flavor of your choice, such as chamomile, peppermint, or rooibos)
- 4 cups boiling water
- 1-2 tablespoons erythritol or another sugar substitute (optional)
- Lemon slices or fresh mint (for garnish)

Instructions:

1. **Steep the Tea:**
   Place the tea bags in a heatproof pitcher. Pour the boiling water over the tea bags and let steep for 5-7 minutes, depending on your desired strength. Remove the tea bags and discard.

2. **Sweeten (Optional):**
   If you prefer a sweeter tea, stir in erythritol or your chosen sugar substitute while the tea is still warm. Adjust to taste.
3. **Chill:**
   Allow the tea to cool to room temperature. Refrigerate until chilled, about 1-2 hours.
4. **Serve:**
   Serve over ice with lemon slices or fresh mint, if desired.

Flavor Variations:

1. Mint-Lemon Iced Tea:

- Use peppermint tea bags. After brewing, add a few fresh mint leaves and lemon slices to the pitcher for extra flavor.

2. Berry Hibiscus Iced Tea:

- Use hibiscus tea bags. After brewing, add a handful of fresh or frozen berries (such as raspberries or blueberries) to the pitcher.

3. Ginger Peach Iced Tea:

- Use a mix of ginger and peach herbal tea bags. Add a few slices of fresh ginger and peach to the pitcher after brewing.

4. Cinnamon Apple Iced Tea:

- Use apple-cinnamon tea bags. After brewing, add a few slices of fresh apple and a cinnamon stick to the pitcher.

Nutritional Information (Per 8 oz serving, plain):

- **Calories:** ~0
- **Protein:** ~0g
- **Carbohydrates:** ~0g
- **Fiber:** ~0g
- **Sugars:** ~0g

Herbal iced teas are a versatile and healthy way to stay hydrated. Customize them with your favorite flavors and garnishes for a refreshing and enjoyable beverage.

Freshly Squeezed Lemon Water

Freshly squeezed lemon water is a simple, refreshing, and healthy drink that's perfect for hydrating and adding a burst of flavor to your water. It's an excellent way to enjoy the benefits of lemon without added sugars or artificial flavors.

Ingredients:

- 1 lemon, freshly squeezed
- 2 cups cold water
- Ice cubes (optional)
- Lemon slices (for garnish, optional)

- Fresh mint leaves (for garnish, optional)

Instructions:

1. **Squeeze the Lemon:**
   Cut the lemon in half and use a citrus reamer or juicer to extract the juice into a small bowl, removing any seeds.
2. **Combine and Stir:**
   In a pitcher or glass, combine the freshly squeezed lemon juice with the cold water. Stir well to mix.
3. **Chill (Optional):**
   Add ice cubes to the pitcher or glass if you prefer your lemon water chilled.
4. **Garnish and Serve:**
   Garnish with lemon slices or fresh mint leaves if desired. Serve immediately or refrigerate for later use.

Nutritional Information (Per 8 oz serving):

- **Calories:** ~6
- **Protein:** ~0g
- **Carbohydrates:** ~2g
- **Fiber:** ~0g
- **Sugars:** ~2g

This *Freshly Squeezed Lemon Water* is a great way to stay hydrated while enjoying the light, tangy flavor of lemon. It's also a refreshing alternative to plain water and can be enjoyed throughout the day.

Low-Sugar Smoothies

Low-sugar smoothies are a great way to enjoy a nutritious and satisfying drink without overloading on sugar. Here are a few recipes that use low-sugar fruits and vegetables to keep the sweetness in check while delivering a delicious flavor and plenty of nutrients.

1. Green Berry Smoothie

Ingredients:

- 1 cup unsweetened almond milk (or any low-carb milk)
- 1/2 cup frozen blueberries
- 1/2 cup fresh spinach or kale
- 1/2 avocado
- 1 tablespoon chia seeds
- 1/2 teaspoon lemon juice
- A few ice cubes (optional)

Instructions:

1. Combine all ingredients in a blender.
2. Blend until smooth. Add ice if you prefer a colder smoothie.
3. Pour into a glass and serve immediately.

2. Cucumber Melon Smoothie

Ingredients:

- 1 cup cucumber, peeled and chopped
- 1/2 cup cantaloupe or honeydew melon
- 1/2 cup unsweetened Greek yogurt
- 1 tablespoon fresh lime juice
- A few fresh mint leaves
- A few ice cubes (optional)

Instructions:

1. Place all ingredients in a blender.
2. Blend until smooth. Add ice for a thicker texture if desired.
3. Serve immediately, garnished with a mint leaf if desired.

3. Strawberry Basil Smoothie

Ingredients:

- 1 cup unsweetened almond milk
- 1/2 cup frozen strawberries
- 1/2 small banana (for sweetness, optional)
- 1 tablespoon fresh basil leaves
- 1 tablespoon flaxseeds
- A few ice cubes (optional)

Instructions:

1. Add all ingredients to a blender.
2. Blend until smooth, adjusting the thickness with ice if needed.

3. Pour into a glass and enjoy!

4. Avocado Coconut Smoothie

Ingredients:

- 1 cup unsweetened coconut milk
- 1/2 avocado
- 1/2 cup frozen raspberries
- 1 tablespoon unsweetened shredded coconut
- 1 tablespoon chia seeds
- A few ice cubes (optional)

Instructions:

1. Blend all ingredients until smooth.
2. Adjust the thickness with ice if desired.
3. Serve immediately.

Nutritional Information (Approximate per serving, varies by recipe):

- **Calories:** ~150-200
- **Protein:** ~4-7g
- **Carbohydrates:** ~12-20g
- **Fiber:** ~4-7g
- **Sugars:** ~6-10g

These *Low-Sugar Smoothies* are designed to be delicious and nutritious while keeping sugar content low. They're perfect for a refreshing breakfast, snack, or post-workout treat.

4o mini
Spiced Almond Milk
ChatGPT

Spiced Almond Milk

Spiced Almond Milk is a warm, comforting beverage that combines the creamy richness of almond milk with aromatic spices. It's perfect for a cozy treat or a soothing drink before bed.

Ingredients:

- 2 cups unsweetened almond milk
- 1/2 teaspoon ground cinnamon
- 1/4 teaspoon ground nutmeg
- 1/4 teaspoon ground ginger
- 1-2 tablespoons erythritol or another sugar substitute (optional, to taste)
- 1/2 teaspoon vanilla extract
- A pinch of sea salt

Instructions:

1. **Heat the Almond Milk:**
   In a small saucepan, heat the almond milk over medium heat until warm but not boiling.
2. **Add Spices:**
   Stir in the ground cinnamon, nutmeg, ginger, and sea salt. If using, add erythritol or your preferred sugar substitute to taste.

3. **Simmer:**
   Continue to heat the mixture, stirring frequently, for about 2-3 minutes to allow the spices to fully blend and the almond milk to become fragrant.
4. **Add Vanilla Extract:**
   Remove the saucepan from heat and stir in the vanilla extract.
5. **Serve:**
   Pour the spiced almond milk into mugs. Serve warm, and enjoy!

Nutritional Information (Per 1 cup serving):

- **Calories:** ~35
- **Protein:** ~1g
- **Carbohydrates:** ~1g
- **Fiber:** ~0g
- **Sugars:** ~0g
- **Fat:** ~2.5g

This *Spiced Almond Milk* is a flavorful, low-calorie drink that's great for warming up on a cool day or adding a touch of spice to your routine. It's also easily customizable with your favorite spices and sweeteners.

Conclusion

Thank you for exploring the world of delicious and health-conscious recipes with us. From vibrant smoothies and satisfying snacks to comforting meals and delightful desserts, these recipes are designed to fit seamlessly into a balanced lifestyle. Each dish focuses on using fresh, wholesome ingredients to enhance flavor while maintaining a mindful approach to nutrition.

Whether you're managing specific dietary needs or simply seeking tasty, nutritious options, these recipes offer a variety of choices to keep your meals exciting and satisfying. Embrace the joy of cooking with these recipes, and enjoy the benefits of a healthier, more delicious way of living.

Printed in Great Britain
by Amazon